UNDERESTIMATED

UNLEASHING THE POWER
OF HIDDEN POTENTIAL

Timothy Hodges

Copyright © 2024 Timothy Hodges
All rights reserved
First Edition

PAGE PUBLISHING
Conneaut Lake, PA

First originally published by Page Publishing 2024

ISBN 979-8-89315-257-9 (pbk)
ISBN 979-8-89315-258-6 (digital)

Printed in the United States of America

This book is a collection of thoughts, ideas, affirmations, advice, and experiences centered around successful leadership, career development, resilience, change, culture, employee recruitment and engagement, and other content devoted to helping others bring out the best in themselves to excel in their careers.

It was written over a two-year period and curated solely from experiences in my professional life. This book is intended to assist and inspire readers in tapping into and finding their authentic voices, inner resiliency, and ambition, and to guide them in realizing a complete and fulfilled life and career.

I toyed with titling this book *Trial and Error* but thought it did not capture the spirit of the content. But the truth is, the information contained in this book is all learned through my experience and the challenges I have overcome, such as being underestimated and then finally becoming unleashed from the insecurities and roadblocks that I put up in my own mind, as many people do.

As a result, I have enjoyed an extremely rewarding career in business, which has been mostly in the health-care industry, even with all the hurdles and dark periods. Now, I am enjoying an even more exciting phase of my life and a new chapter as an entrepreneur.

I didn't get to this better place easily, and I have been lucky enough to collect some wisdom and lessons along the way. These lessons were mostly learned from the twists and turns, good mentors, falling down, and getting back up after falling down.

I guess you could consider much of the content in this book as war stories. Luckily for me, I am still here, stronger and a little smarter as a result. I hope to pass on some helpful tidbits that will get you where you are headed faster and better prepared than I was.

The essence of teamwork

In your career, it's important to know the difference between how far you can take something and how far things can go. Individuals can only take things to a certain level. I believe it takes a team, good leadership, and vision to take things as far as they can go.

Reaching the summit

There are mountains we are forced to climb and mountains we choose to climb. Both can be challenging for quite different reasons. Ultimately, the one thing both scenarios have in common is that when you reach the top of the mountain, the accomplishment you achieve is extremely rewarding. So keep climbing.

Talk about leadership confidence

The best boss that I ever had told me her goal was for me to take over her position one day, and eventually go further than she did in her own career. She made both happen. I am forever grateful to her. These are the types of leaders you want to work for, and the type of leader you should strive to be.

Here's an idea

One key management concept that I learned over time is that when an employee has an idea or makes a decision, let them run with it. As a leader and manager, you don't need to love every idea or even fully support every decision that your team members make. However, the likelihood of an idea or decision being a success is greatly enhanced when your team members have total ownership of them, because they are 100 percent their ideas. Also, if the idea flops or a decision they make is not successful, never second guess them. That is the kiss of death for the trust between a manager and a team member.

Play the long game…

Just remember on challenging days that you don't need to win every game in the regular season to get to the World Series. You just need to win the most.

The luck of the draw

>When it comes to success:
>Experience truly matters,
>Strong leadership skills are essential,
>A good work ethic is key,
>Knowledge is power,
>Teamwork and diversity are critical,
>And staying humble is a must.
>But…
>Timing is everything.

Earn it!

I have always believed that if you have to ask people to respect you, it will never happen. Respect should occur organically because of a person's character, integrity, and knowledge. It really must be earned over time and naturally through actions and behaviors that warrant true respect.

Myth buster…

One of the best salespeople that I know recently told me that she "doesn't think of herself as a salesperson." I told her that is what I think makes her great. The best salespeople don't realize they are actually selling; they are just being themselves, authentic.

Simple ingredients for success...

Below are values I try hard to follow daily. I don't always get it right, nobody is perfect, but having this plan and guide helps keep things in focus:
Be opportunistic, not greedy,
Competitive, not cutthroat,
Ambitious, but balanced,
Decisive, but thoughtful,
Assertive, not aggressive,
Determined, but not tone-deaf,
Driven, but inclusive,
Growth-oriented, but grateful for all that you have achieved.

No matter how big or small...

I have learned early on in business that you treat your smallest accounts with the same attention, respect, sense of urgency, and priority as your largest clients. It's the bulletproof approach to building and sustaining a successful business.

New actions, new outcomes...

A good rule of thumb in marketing and business overall is that if you don't act on new ideas, don't expect new results.

Looking in the mirror

I have come to appreciate that in marketing and business development, the most important question to ask yourself frequently is, "What do people know you and your company for?"

Asking this question often and knowing the answer, especially in relation to your competitors, are the keys to growth in your business and are necessary to achieving the highest market share.

Own it!

I have worked in both great and not-so-great company cultures in my career. What I have found to be true is that companies who spend a lot of time talking about and selling a great culture actually aren't so great. Meanwhile, those that actually spend time working to make a culture great truly are.

Fixing a flat tire

The worst interview question of all time I believe is, "What are your weaknesses?"

First, people generally don't know or think a lot about what their weaknesses are. Second, if they do, they are certainly not going to raise a red flag in an interview about themselves. Finally, what can an interviewer really do with the answers people give?

I have substituted this question during interviews with, "Can you share with me what professional development goals you have for yourself?"

I have had success with this in gaining better insight, and people tend to open up more. This question makes for a more pleasant interview experience for the candidate overall. And I think everyone would agree that is the goal of an interview.

Hopping and shopping

What I once used to consider "job hopping," I now see as "employer shopping."

As the need and quest for talent has undergone a seismic shift in the past few years, many employees are sampling, trialing, and assessing the culture of new employers to gauge if they are a good fit in the long haul. It is not unusual or negative these days to see employees who have been at one, two, or even three companies in the past couple of years.

What I hear the most from candidates now is, "I am looking for a home." Similarly, I am finding employers are okay with trying different things with candidates and are open to new styles of and approaches to leadership and management.

Savvy employers know they have to adapt to this new transitory mindset. Job candidates should not be insecure about having held a few positions within a brief time frame, and employers should be open to this new dynamic and should not eliminate a candidate because of this. As an employer, you may be the home that many high-quality candidates have been seeking.

Take a broader view

A key management concept that often gets overlooked is, "Never gauge the performance of a team member based on a moment in time. Base your opinion on their body of work over a period of time." This is not always the easiest thing to do, but the healthiest and right mindset for any success-driven leader and organization.

Both sides of the same coin

I have been on both sides of this. Younger managers often complain that when they become supervisors to individuals older than them, the older employees treat them like they don't know what they are doing because they are younger. More seasoned team members complain that younger leaders don't respect their years of experience.

The solution? If you are the younger manager, take the opportunity to learn from those who have more experience than you, you don't know everything. To the more seasoned team members, embrace new ideas and new perspectives; you don't know everything.

Are we there yet?

You may not have found your voice yet. But when you do, you will know it. It is all about knowing exactly what you stand for, passionately believe in, support, will not compromise on, and the talents you have. You can use these factors to make a difference to benefit others. You will know when you have found it.

In fact, it's inside of you right now, you just have to allow yourself to tap into it

Building the plane while it's flying

I sometimes chuckle to myself when I hear companies discussing onboarding, training, and orientation of new employees. Don't get me wrong, I wholeheartedly believe a thorough orientation and training is key to an employee's success.

I do remember, though, my first day as a new sales employee at a large company many years ago. I met with my supervisor and regional manager for an "orientation." They spent ten minutes describing the role and the company, and then said to me, "Now go and make something happen." I wound up loving the company and staying for eight years.

In a sense, figuring out things for yourself sometimes is the most beneficial orientation one can receive.

Don't sweet-talk me

When someone resigns, it is not uncommon for a manager to start "sweet-talking" the employee into staying. A manager can offer promises of promotions, new glamorous titles, a commitment to making changes, a salary increase, etc.

But the question always is, "Why now? Why all the attention and affection now that the person resigned? Why did it take a resignation to receive all this kindness?" The answer is because they resigned, and the manager is afraid to lose the employee!

Companies with a healthy culture recognize and address employees' concerns, frustrations, and development needs as they occur, not when everything is on the line at the eleventh hour. Remember that if you are ever on the receiving end of the sweet talk.

But also remember that no company is perfect, and even the best companies and managers make mistakes. More often than not, they deserve a second chance, and at the very least, your open mind to what they have to say.

A change of heart

Job hunters! If you accept a position, and then decide to back out, do it quickly. Backing out of a position one or two weeks before you start is very unprofessional and unfair to the employer you committed to.

Things happen, that is understandable, but you can guarantee to burn a bridge with a prospective employer when you rescind your acceptance close to your start date. You never know when you may need that employer again or where the people you deal with in these situations may wind up in the future.

The succession dilemma...

I received good advice many years ago from a human resources manager I worked with. She advised me to never let a superstar choose their replacement when they leave a position regardless of whether they are leaving for a promotion, another department, or leaving the company altogether.

Her theory was that a successful person exiting a role is not objective enough to choose someone who can potentially perform better than they did. I've always followed that rule, and it has always worked for me.

With great power, comes great responsibility

I think a lot about the responsibility seasoned managers have in developing people who are early in their careers. I can't believe sometimes how much management, mentoring, and development I received in my 20s and 30s continue to be useful today in my 50s. I think we sometimes forget how much of an impact we can make in shaping future managers and leaders. It really is a gift we are given and not to be taken for granted.

More doesn't always mean better

When I was in sales and marketing, I never really made an impact on business development until I realized that the quality of client relationships far outweighs the quantity of client relationships.

I scream, you scream…

Work ethic—we learn it from somewhere. Every year in mid-July, I think about my first job at Carvel ice cream when I was sixteen years old. I asked my father if I could go to my first concert to see Fleetwood Mac, and he said yes, on the condition that I find a job and buy the tickets myself.

So I slugged ice cream all summer at one of their busiest stores. I probably made $6 an hour as I recall. I saved up, bought two tickets for me and my older sister (she was my ride and the person responsible for introducing me to a lot of good music).

The concert was incredible. The next day, I told my parents how much fun we had. My father said, "If you want nice things in life, you have to work for them." A valuable lesson that helped shape the rest of my life.

As a result, I've never not had a job since I was sixteen. I am forever grateful for this and the countless other lessons my parents taught me. By the way, I tip really well whenever I get ice cream now at any ice cream shop. That job was no joke and definitely hard work!

Let's put things in perspective

I find people increasingly judgmental on social media. To start with, it's social media, not rocket science or brain surgery. Let's put things in perspective with everything that is going on in the world.

If you don't like something you see, scroll past it and move on. What one person may view as annoying or not worthy of putting out there, someone else may find great meaning and value in. Good content is in the eye of the beholder. Let's all try to be good with that.

You clean up well

When people ask me for advice on companies to work for, I tell them what matters most to me.

Assess a company not on how well they avoid problems from happening but rather how quickly and thoroughly they fix problems when they do arise.

Problems are inevitable in every industry, every company. Those organizations that shine in taking care of issues are the ones I appreciate the most and who typically have the most longevity and success.

First and lasting impressions

Early in my career, I received the first call from my new supervisor who just replaced a boss that I was very fond of. Five minutes into the conversation, he said he was calling to discuss a "significant issue."

He proceeded to ask me why I hadn't taken a vacation in over a year. I gave him all the type A, ambitious answers. I am too busy, I love what I do, I don't need a vacation, too much piles up when you go away, blah, blah, blah.

He shared with me that he needed focus, drive, and results from his team. To give those, he needed me to also be balanced and to appreciate life outside of work.

I was stunned and thought he was joking, actually. But he wasn't, and I was completely taken off guard. He did things like this often in the few years I worked for him, and we had a great rapport and accomplished a lot.

Not only was his philosophy right on the mark, but what a clever way to establish an immediate positive impression as a new supervisor on an employee. In my mind, I was thinking, *This guy just took on this huge position, and he's worried I need to have more balance? Immediate respect for him!*

A great lesson for me that I try to pay forward as much as possible.

Every company's aspiration

Tesla doesn't really advertise. Their strategy is to create demand and brand loyalty via exceptional quality and innovation. It looks like it's working.

There's no ceiling on growth

I am forever thinking of ways to grow and improve, even on the back nine of my career. I often jot down reminders to myself of what is important in achieving success, even after thirty-plus years in the workforce. I am nerdy that way. Here are some of those reminders:

- No goals, no success.
- Hire the best people, even if they are at the top of your budget.
- Create an environment for success for those people.
- Be your own worst critic.
- Love your clients.
- Let go of setbacks quickly.
- Learn from setbacks quickly.
- Celebrate success but also move on quickly from those.
- Give your team credit for all successes, take none for yourself.
- Don't be a yesterday person, be a tomorrow person.
- Listen more than you speak.
- Take time every day for yourself and your family.
- Count your blessings daily.

A gentle reminder

I recently stuck a note on my desktop in my office to remind me to not get too caught up in the minutia of every day. It has been working. I think it's important to focus on macro things often, they can get lost unless you remind yourself of how valuable they are.

The note I posted on my computer reads:

Big Picture, Big Picture, Big Picture.

It's not what you know…

Success and longevity in any career or leadership role have so much to do with your ability to effectively communicate information. I have seen brilliant people who are extremely intelligent and experts in their subject matter plateau and grow stagnant due to an inability to communicate what they know to help others learn and develop.

Knowledge is power, but it is also not worth much unless it can be effectively shared.

Tell it like it is

I have always preferred managers and leaders who are direct, even when that directness can be uncomfortable to hear. I have also seen the opposite…managers who are not direct or transparent. Those who smile, project a warm and friendly personality on the surface in public, and then turn around and be ruthless toward people behind their back. These managers, to me, are far worse than those with an honest and direct approach.

It's always best to know where you stand with leaders and to work with people who share honest opinions and feedback.

Multiple choice

There are three types of business leaders. The first type likes to start companies and be entrepreneurs.

The second type is attracted to growing businesses.

And the third seeks out fix-it turnaround situations.

The key to success in your career is to understand which one of these bests describes you.

A hard habit to break

I have a bad habit professionally of not keeping in touch as much as I should with people that I have worked with in the past.

I am constantly working on that, and I appreciate people who have that trait.

I tend to be a tomorrow person instead of a yesterday person; but as I get older, I realize increasingly how important prior connections and history are in a person's success and fulfillment.

Try to stay in touch with people you value. Your professional network never can be full enough of fans, wisdom, and inspiring people!

The success equation

In my humble opinion, here's the success equation:
Success =
1 percent Fate
1 percent Karma
1 percent Luck
97 percent Taking initiative

Think about this

I believe the two most important self-care tips in business to focus on are:

- Your brain, so you are always thinking wisely and clearly.
- Your spine, so you never lose your conviction, courage, and credibility.

For your reference

I am sure I am not the only one who has experienced this…

I receive more calls from people asking me for references and opinions on job candidates who do not list me as a reference vs. people calling for a reference where I was actually listed as a reference!

Informal reference checking is fairly common. However, it is also a great reminder to be conscious of your professional relationships and the importance of having a credible reputation in business and maintaining regular contact or repair with colleagues that people associate you with.

Learn by doing

I don't have any regrets professionally, but I do have areas that I wish I focused more on in my career. Below are some of those things. Although they are still a focus for me professionally, and I've actually made progress in the past few years, I wish I had worked harder in these areas earlier on in my career.

Do the following resonate with you?

1. Underestimating others' talent and abilities often (as well as my own)
2. Not reflecting enough on failures and successes
3. Holding and attending too many meetings
4. Not seeking feedback enough as a manager or leader
5. Focusing too much on business metrics, not enough on culture
6. Not providing constructive feedback to others as often as I should have
7. Having a healthier personal and professional balance
8. Having more patience
9. Not spending enough time to focus on strategic initiatives vs. lost in the day-to-day
10. Not enough time spent on recognizing and celebrating other's accomplishments

It's healthy to take inventory on where you want to develop professionally, no matter what stage you are at in your career. Some advice…reflect more often than you are currently doing, and more often than you think you need to.

Can you hear me now?

I was recently reminded of a simple, yet fundamental shift in management style that has impacted my professional life and business results. I enjoy few things more than meeting with leadership and department heads in the companies I consult and advise for.

After a few get-togethers recently, I was reminded how rewarding and impactful it is to ask questions and hear what people have to say—their ideas, challenges, perspectives, and needs.

To be honest, fifteen years ago, I entered most meetings, talked or presented for an hour or so, and accomplished very little. There is nothing more powerful in building culture and success in business than allowing the people who actually do the work to inform decision-makers about what needs to be done and what they need from you to get there.

Sinking and swimming

I was recently with a physician and a sales representative who is early in her career and working for a company I consulted with to help them grow market share. The sales representative was describing the services offered by her company to the physician. She presented all the specialty programs the company has, the referral process, the organization overview, etc.

The physician politely paused her and asked, "Sounds great, but how is your company doing with patient outcomes and care day-to-day?"

He wanted real-world and actual patient testimonials and outcomes. He didn't care about the elaborate marketing materials and power point presentation.

The sales representative didn't skip a beat and proceeded to do an excellent job addressing the specifics he wanted, and the physician was satisfied.

However, there is a lesson here. I could have jumped in early in the conversation to avoid the frustration I was sensing from the physician; I saw where things were going. I think, though, that would have embarrassed the sales representative. But she will never forget the question the physician asked her, and she will improve and grow as a result.

Sometimes, the best teaching and mentoring is when you don't throw a lifeline to someone and allow them to learn naturally.

To do this, you must have good judgment to not allow things to go so far that they are unsalvageable—not only in sales but also in any area of operation. But people who are flying without a net will more often than not find a soft place to land.

Learning as we go along

A good sign that you are getting wiser in your career journey is when the first few items on your daily to-do list are self-care items before you get to the business to-do items.

Can you tell one from another?

Sometimes in business, arrogance gets mistaken as confidence, and vice versa. Honestly, I have learned this by trial and error in my own career. Below is what I believe distinguishes one from another in a person:

Confidence: Speaking your mind to help a situation.
Arrogance: Speaking for attention seeking purposes.

Confidence: Listening and accepting input from your team.
Arrogance: Not listening or open to other viewpoints.

Confidence: Being compromise-oriented.
Arrogance: "My way or the highway."

Confidence: Making a point with facts that support your point.
Arrogance: "Because I said so" mindset.

Confidence: Conceding for the greater good when needed.
Arrogance: Holding a grudge.

Confidence: Giving credit where credit is due.
Arrogance: Always taking the credit for yourself.

Confidence: Admitting mistakes.
Arrogance: Never being wrong.

Confidence: Hiring people as strong or stronger than you are.
Arrogance: Hiring beneath you for fear of being eclipsed.

Confidence: Not wavering in your values and principles.
Arrogance: Committing to something you don't believe in.

Seeking humility

It has and will continue to be a job searchers market for an extended period of time. No matter how hot the market is for job seekers, though, it is important to remain humble, grateful, and earnest in interviews and in the recruitment process with the people interested in hiring you.

Things can change on a dime and quickly reverse to opportunities drying up and the job market cooling off. I have seen it happen many times in my career. There is a fine line between being confident in your marketability and worth as a candidate and being pompous and difficult to work with. Try to stay conscious of that.

Regardless of how many opportunities are available these days, those who conduct themselves professionally and with integrity, and exhibit basic manners in the recruitment process, always make out the best in the long run.

Sixth sense

Intuition is underrated. Try to surround yourself as much as possible with people who have above average intuition. These individuals will help you achieve success and offer clear perspectives more than anyone.

Seeing is believing

Most people know great leadership when they see it, because most people know or have seen poor leadership also at some point in their careers.

No better time than the present

I don't believe in annual employee evaluations. I have always strived to provide feedback and constructive suggestions to direct reports routinely and in real time. Waiting a year to discuss an employee's strengths, opportunities for improvement, and career growth is irresponsible.

Evaluating compensation annually, yes. Performance discussions, though, should be fluid and ongoing. People appreciate knowing where they stand at all times, especially if retention and morale are important to a company culture.

Social distortion

Social media is a great vehicle for businesses to share, learn, connect, etc. It's also good, I think, to save a little bit for yourself and feel no pressure to share everything.

When you share everything on social media, it doesn't leave anything special for the special people in your professional life to know or learn about you or your business. A lot of posts I read on social media are TMI, but maybe it's a generational thing?

Quitting is such sweet sorrow

I have always believed that there is a big difference between quitting a job and knowing when to cut your losses and moving on from a position or company.

Quitting implies giving up, cutting your losses means you are getting off a sinking ship, which implies character and intelligence. In speaking with job candidates throughout my career, I often feel compelled to share this thought with them when they say, "I am not a quitter," when they are struggling with leaving a position. I think this distinction gives people clarity and permission to look at changing jobs in a healthier and more beneficial way.

Note to self

I'm a huge proponent for higher education. Although I am grateful for the privilege of the education I have received, it hasn't prepared me for everything.

If you aspire to receive a promotion, or want to be a supervisor, manager, director, or to elevate to the "C suite," I have learned that the following skills are critical, and you will not read them in a textbook:

- Knowing when a member of your team needs help, and helping them;
- Understanding the difference between challenging individuals to achieve their best potential vs. pushing them too hard;
- Communicating complex information that a broad audience can easily digest and understand;
- Knowing when to listen more than speaking;
- Creating and sustaining a culture of ideas and sharing opinions, especially ones that differ from yours;
- Being thoughtful to people daily and showing appreciation consistently;
- Inspiring your direct reports and teams to enjoy the art and spirit of always being aware of external competition and encouraging them to stay ahead of it.

The list of real-world leadership lessons goes on and on. These are just a few that I have been reminded of recently. I still find tremendous value in striving to accomplish all of these.

I have had the good fortune to help build a very large company in my career from the ground up. One of my major lessons in this process was learning you cannot build on a flawed foundation. *How* you grow in business is equally as important as *how much* you grow your business.

Phone a friend

A colleague recently called me and said she was "stuck," feeling stagnant, and was seeking advice on how to snap out of it. I asked how things were going performance wise at work, and she said, "Awesome." There were really no issues or anything she was overly worried about in terms of job stability, and her company seemed happy with her performance.

I told her she might be mistaking or confusing not having a huge problem or not being in some work-related crisis with being "stuck."

Many type A people have a tough time accepting and enjoying their own success and can't relate well to the few times when things are smooth sailing for them.

I advised her to enjoy the moment, and that I didn't think she was stagnant, but rather not used to taking a deep breath and acknowledging her hard won successes.

It's not complacency to enjoy stability, it's healthy. Just don't get "stuck" there either.

A word to the wise

A wise manager taught me a long time ago to never begin an employee evaluation with negative feedback. No matter how good or tough the evaluation is, always begin them with positive feedback and dialogue.

The theory is that the person receiving the evaluation will not remember or hear anything you say after negative or constructive feedback is shared. That person will walk away defeated with no recall of anything positive. It was a great suggestion, and it has never failed to work for me.

A common thread

No matter who you admire, who you report to, who inspires you, who you disregard, who you think is perfect, who your peers are, who you supervise, who you mentor, who mentors you, etc., they all have one thing in common:

At some point in their careers, they have had tough setbacks and failures. Keep this in mind whenever you are going through a challenging time or situation. You are not alone. It's not just you. Everyone around you has been there; they have all survived and will probably be there again at some point.

I will add they have all also grown as a result of surviving these situations, and so will you.

Apples and oranges

Growth and change are distinctly different. I often hear people say, "I can't change who I am," when confronting a challenge or a new situation. But you really don't have to ever change who you are.

Change is becoming someone who you are not.

Growth is improving upon the someone you already are.

Be open-minded to feedback and situations that encourage and force you to grow. You will know when you are experiencing this by the number one signal…you are starting to feel uncomfortable in your comfort zone.

I'm just putting it out there…

I have learned not to get too attached to a new idea just because it is my idea. I have trained myself at this point to ask people not if they like a new idea; rather, here's my idea, what do you suggest we do to make the idea better?

It's a productive and inclusive exercise and always takes new ideas to a level I wouldn't be able to take them to on my own.

A different lens

When someone you respect sees something in you that you don't, trust them. Eventually you will see it for yourself.

Nothing has changed

When I worked full time as an employee for someone else, I used to pride myself on approaching everything I did as if I also owned the company.

Now that I own my company, I don't really work any differently or harder, because my work ethic has never changed. If you are all in on your job, your company, your career, etc., you will always succeed, regardless if the company is yours or not.

Cancel my subscription

Dreams don't come true organically. Dreams are another word for goals, and goals are achieved by working hard toward them with people you trust and believe in, and those who share a common vision.

I don't subscribe to the mindset I see often from motivational gurus that if you *will* something, then it must come true. Aspire, yes; have a positive attitude, yes; wishing and hoping success into existence, not so much.

In a perfect world or an alternate universe, that might happen. In the real world, however, accomplishments require a huge amount of effort, determination, and hard work.

You are seen

Don't get discouraged if you feel you are not getting credit for the work that you do. Even when you don't think so, in a healthy company, the leadership is almost always aware of who the drivers of results and success are.

I've seen this over and over. People see you; they know you, and they are aware of your accomplishments and contributions. You will see…

And if they don't, you have some tough decisions to make.

It's (mostly) out of your hands

You can't create or manufacture your own reputation in business. The people you work with create it for you. However, you can help shape your reputation by how you treat people and the quality of your work.

Something's gotta give

I know this is management and leadership 101, but if you expect a strong work ethic and elevated performance from your team, you have to demonstrate the same qualities and behaviors to them as a leader.

Shaken, not stirred

"Why don't we try this?"

These are five especially important words in the business world. If you find yourself saying this a lot, you are a natural-born leader because you are prone to constructive problem-solving.

If you find yourself hearing this a lot, you're a natural-born leader because you are surrounding yourself with other solution-oriented team members.

If you don't say or hear this often, you may want to consider shaking things up a little. It may mean you or the team need some help with embracing change and innovation.

Turns out, your parents were right

Good manners matter…

People notice when a person is polite, respectful, and well mannered, and it really counts. They also notice when they don't see it.

Sometimes we overthink about what it takes to make a positive impression. All things being equal…genuine gestures, actions, and nuances often make a big difference in helping a person and their company stand out from the rest of the pack.

Changing lanes

Move out of your team's way and let them take things in a direction you cannot or have not imagined. Projects, ideas, programs, etc. Incredible results can occur with this approach.

Letting go of control does not always mean the end of something, it often marks the beginning of something better.

The glass is half full

Understand your worth! What one employer may not recognize, think they need, take for granted, or value in you, potential new employers may desire greatly and have a tremendous need for!

Be careful what you dream of

The work and endurance that it takes to succeed is nothing compared to what it takes to maintain that success. Know your competition inside and out, but ultimately the toughest competition is with yourself.

DNA test

Once you start viewing challenges and problems as opportunities to grow, you begin to see what you are really made of.

A good tip

I am out at business meals at least two to three times per week. I always take care of the check as much as possible. I just think it's classy and a nice reflection of who you are, even if the other person has initiated the meeting.

I also learned from a mentor to give my credit card to the host or hostess when entering the restaurant to avoid the uncomfortable tug of war scenario with check at the end of the meal.

I also think it's important to tip well always and suggest 25 percent minimally (20 percent is now considered just okay) especially if it's a place you frequent for business. The staff notice kindness and will make sure you and your guests are well attended to.

Also, most places pool their tips, so one bad encounter with one person shouldn't ruin things for the entire staff. Most business associates you dine with notice all these things. If you want to get to know someone well in business, there is a lot you can glean from their interactions with personnel at a restaurant, and their professional etiquette at a business meal.

We've all been there

Don't worry if you feel a little unsure, insecure, uneasy, and curious at times in your career. It usually indicates that you are not a person who can tolerate always moving in the same direction unless that direction is forward.

Be concerned if you are *not* experiencing these feelings, no one ever grows without realizing first they need to.

Right here, right now

Try to live as much as possible in the moment. You can learn from the past, but you can't change it. You can plan for the future, but you can't predict what it holds.

Theres no better time to get things done and pursue fulfillment than right now…today.

A great twist of fate

Align with people who have big ideas, plans, and ambition. But make sure they also have a big and caring heart, and you will be well cared for. If you do this, there's a good chance that someday you will become that person for others.

Toxic area! Keep out!

I am often speaking with individuals about their careers, their future, and where they want to go professionally. I frequently share with them that you can have a great job in a company with a toxic culture, and a not-so-great job in a company with a great culture.

In great cultures, there is an exceptionally good probability that job satisfaction can improve. Both can be challenging situations, but make no mistake about it. Toxic cultures almost never improve.

It's all your choice

We often become the people who have mentored, managed, and trained us in our careers. So be selective and thoughtful about who you choose to work for and who you allow to influence your professional skills, your style, and your leadership ability. The key here is knowing that you can choose.

Can you spare some changing

The best things in life are always free, even in our professional lives. Things that cost nothing that go a long way with teammates and associates:

- Thanking
- Complimenting
- Encouraging
- Sharing
- Smiling

- Listening
- Motivating
- Supporting
- Collaborating
- Teaching

No short cuts in business

The people who we admire the most, the ones who make everything seem effortless…they have actually been working, tweaking, practicing, and refining their skills over many years through trial and error.

There truly is no such thing as an overnight success.

For what it's worth

Always expect to be paid what you're worth, but never at the expense of your self-worth.

Paybacks are a blessing

Pay back those who took an interest in you and your career by paying forward the same kindness and attention to those who need the same from you.

Stay connected

The most effective marketing is when a company expresses their culture from the inside out, and then provides an opportunity for their customers to make a connection with them.

The greater good

You can be a fierce competitor in the industry or profession you are in, while also being a fierce advocate for the industry you are in. The two are not mutually exclusive.

Two are better than one

Knowledge + effective communication skills = an unstoppable person.
But one without the other is meaningless.

This will not go unnoticed

More than anything, people notice those who try the most.
They notice when you show up for a ½ hour meeting after driving two hours. They notice if you follow up or follow through on the smallest details even when you are incredibly busy. They notice when you give of yourself when you have nothing to gain from it.
And they notice when you give your all to something important to the company, even when the outcome is unknown.

Leaning in, literally

Achieving results is often about using good old-fashioned "elbow grease." No matter what industry or position you have.
Data, spreadsheets, reports, meetings, and algorithms often become useless.
There are more times than not when there simply is no substitute for rolling up our sleeves, getting our boots on the ground, and supporting our coworkers and teams while we learn something new in the process.

Codependency

The architect is nothing without the builder, the builder is nothing without the architect.

Going somewhere

I have hired a lot of people who on paper were not the "perfect" candidates, but turned out to be superstars. I think it's key when interviewing people to focus less on where they have been, and a lot more on where they are headed.

Spring cleaning

Always a good thought to free up as much space in our lives for things that are positive and productive, and to let go of negativity so we can use that space to achieve new goals.

Pick from your own garden

I am certain that any success I have had in my career has had a lot to do with promoting employees from within. People who are nurtured and grown internally in an organization tend to be more motivated, grateful, and loyal.

As a result, these individuals add a huge amount of quality and value to a company's culture and performance.

Emotional intelligence

The pat on the back we get or give when things don't go well is far more meaningful than the one we get or give when everything is perfect.

Inside out

There are times in your career that you may be either an *insider* or an *outsider*.

Outsiders are those who challenge conventional thinking, question the status quo, innovate, disrupt, and often face resistance because they view things differently.

I have always admired outsiders because these individuals are determined, gratified, and enjoy what they are doing. Even in the face of significant adversity.

Ironically, the most successful outsiders eventually become insiders because often, the innovation and change they have worked tirelessly for was so necessary that it becomes the standard in their respective industries.

So here's to the outsiders. Forge ahead. Don't give up, never quit. When you are passionate about positive change and innovation, there is a good chance your way will become the norm.

I don't know who you are anymore

No matter what your job is, where you work, what your circumstances are, or how you are feeling, try to do at least one thing every day that reminds you of who you are, and what you are made of.

Using GPS

A great (and real) description of a leader:
A hundred things are going great.
One thing is not.
Where can the best leaders be found?
Spending time on the one thing that is not working, trying to help make it better.

The $1,000,000 pyramid

How you treat others,
How you react to stress,
What you focus on,
When and how you support others,
What you say,
What you don't say,
How hard you are on yourself,
How much balance you have,
What you say yes to,
What you say no to,
Who you associate yourself with,
How much effort you do or don't give,
How you hold others accountable,

How you hold yourself accountable,
How positive or negative you are.
It's important to remember:
It's all our own choice.

Dig deeper

Success doesn't occur organically. Most successful people I know have been motivated to succeed due to some adversity they experienced in their life.

When you celebrate others' success, you are really celebrating their resilience, their will, and their determination to overcome this adversity. Success is the end result, but the person's story and journey is the real inspiration and what we should learn from the most.

Graceful exits

I always appreciate it when a person who accepts a new position with me is meticulous and thoughtful about how they give notice and the manner in which they exit with their current employer.

I find that people who are concerned about separating from an employer in a good way demonstrate a true sign of professionalism. They are very responsible people.

It also validates that the person is a good hire. I have seen the opposite also. And when you see questionable behavior in this scenario, its usually a red flag.

Winning isn't everything

It's always a challenge for competitive, driven individuals and companies to be good sports in business.

Not winning all the time can be difficult. After many years in business, however, I have come to respect and admire people and companies who move on from failures quickly and who are not sore losers.

Appreciate people and companies who learn from setbacks and failures, they always seem to fare better and win more in the long run.

Natural-born leaders

Breakthrough leadership moments occur when you decide to do what is necessary vs. doing what is popular.

Grin and bear it

Fixing and cleaning up mistakes as a leader is an inevitable part of the job. The best leaders I have worked with, however, not only work hard to fix mistakes, they don't complain while doing it. Even when it's not their mistake to clean up.

Attitude matters.

Stop avoiding me

Life would be great if we could just "wish" difficult situations and tough conversations away.

But we can't.

They have to be confronted head on, and immediately, and without fear. The best motivation to resolve conflict is thinking about the consequences of ignoring conflict. Things become far worse when left unaddressed.

Face the situation, tackle conflict and tough conversations directly, even if it is uncomfortable for you. It is a necessary skill for anyone aspiring to advance in their career.

Deal me in

If you really believe in a person or an idea, double down on them.

Some will test you to gauge how firm and passionate you are in what and who you believe in. It's not often that people are consistent with their convictions. Don't back down, it will surprise those who challenge and doubt you, and reveal your true character to everyone.

Guilty by association

When you tolerate and continue working in a culture that you know is toxic, you are passively endorsing and supporting that culture by staying it.

What you choose to accept and tolerate in your work environment is a direct reflection of your values, and shapes your reputation and the opportunities afforded to you in the industry you work in.

To thy own self be true

You should give as much of yourself to your professional journey as possible. But remembering this is as important:
Know yourself.
Be yourself.
Accept yourself.
Take pride in yourself.
Don't underestimate yourself.
Trust yourself.
Challenge yourself.
Take care of yourself.

Time management

What you know about your industry, and the relationships you develop within your industry, matters more than anyone you are trying to impress and politicking to within the higher ranks of your company.

Spend more time with the employees in the field who make things happen every day, and the customers who support your company. If you do this, the stronger, smarter, and more indispensable you will be.

The starting lineup

An important element of success is to bring the people who were there for you and believed in you on your journey along for the ride. Your supporters deserve to reap the rewards of success for their loyalty and hard work as much as you do!

Be careful what you wish for

The strongest leaders are always given the toughest challenges.
It goes with the territory. And at times it is a very, very large territory.

The waiting game

I would rather keep a position open and find the right candidate, than hire someone who is not top quality to merely fill the position and check off a box.

Aim to hire the highest quality and best people. Never compromise. Bringing on the best people accomplishes three crucial things:

1. The best people improve culture.
2. The best people have elevated expectations of their leaders, they will push you to elevate your own performance as a leader.
3. The best people attract other equally high-caliber people to join your company because they are there.

No shortcuts; hire the best at all costs.

Learn from the best

Steve Jobs has always been a top leadership icon and inspiration to me. One of his most important and underappreciated business decisions was to choose his successor at Apple when he knew his medical condition was terminal.

He chose what many believed was not the most popular or best choice at the time. Tim Cook who succeeded him as CEO is the total opposite of Jobs. Where Jobs was known for his charisma, vision, and marketing prowess, Cook is known for his discipline, transparency, and appreciation of culture.

Jobs' brilliance in selecting Cook is a testament to his legacy and a good lesson for the rest of us. He knew that to ensure a strong future for Apple, it required a different skill set and leadership style from his.

And that decision in fact did secure his legacy. The company has gone on since Job's departure to reach new highs in market capitalization and market share. It has become, and remains to be, one of the most powerful companies on the planet, thanks to Tim Cook.

The lesson? The best leaders see beyond themselves. They have the foresight to make unselfish decisions, even unpopular decisions, to ensure the best interests of their people and their companies.

Truly inspiring, and a great reminder for anyone who aspires to hold a leadership position.

Turning the ship around

Do you fear public speaking? You are not alone, so did I. In fact, poll after poll indicates that one of the greatest fears of businesspeople and people in general is public speaking.

It was so crippling for me that I would cancel presentations I had to give at my company early in my career (a couple of times calling out sick), would avoid scheduling larger client presentations (keep in mind, I was in sales at the time), and would turn down opportunities to present at industry conferences.

A turning point for me was one day early in my career when I forced myself to present to an audience of nurses about how clinical care has changed and evolved over the years in the inpatient setting. To add insult to injury, there were two people from my corporate office in attendance.

I was a wreck. My hands and voice were shaking, I was sweating, it was my greatest nightmare. And then something life changing occurred. I asked the group a question, abandoned my PowerPoint presentation, and began a dialogue with the group. I completely forgot that I was being evaluated and judged by anyone, lost all fear, and went on to have a successful presentation.

The key? I became comfortable when talking naturally with an audience about subject matter that I knew cold.

I have to pinch myself sometimes today that I give five to ten presentations per month, including keynote addresses and other large group presentations. I still get nervous, but it's a healthy kind of nervous.

If you are fearful of public speaking, you can overcome this. Some things that have worked for me:

- Always speak about what you know well.
- Practice, practice, practice.
- Learn from other speakers you admire and study them well.
- Be your authentic self; don't let a fear of others judging you hold you back. People respect authenticity.
- Seek constructive feedback from people you trust and respect.

There is no greater feeling than the feeling of overcoming something you fear, but you must confront it head on!

Wait a second!

Never second guess a decision that someone you hired has made. If you do this, especially publicly, you've probably lost the person for good, and they will never trust you again.

No problem

I have always found it fairest to evaluate managers and leaders less on *if* problems occur on their watch, but more so on *how* they manage and learn from these problems. I really don't know any environment that is problem free.

Wish list

This is my criteria for people I refer to as my *inner circle*. They are individuals who:

- Share knowledge and advice unselfishly.
- Embrace DEI principles and values.
- Can be introduced to my most important and trusted business contacts.
- Can be counted on when I am at my most vulnerable and not judge me.
- Can forgive me for not being perfect.
- Will allow me to be my authentic self.
- Will challenge me constructively at the right moments.
- I can share ideas with them freely without fear of them stealing or attempting to take credit.
- Are respectful of personal and professional boundaries that are important to me.
- Are not seeking anything in return from me except respect, loyalty, and advice.
- Consistently offer honest, practical feedback, and opinions.
- Can utilize them as a reference without having to tell them.

It's a tall order, but that's why they call it an inner circle. I feel fortunate to have colleagues who exemplify these traits, and I strive to do the same for them.

What do you think?

It seems to me that a lot of successful people in business were born with a gene that allows them to not care about what other people think.

I sometimes wish I had that also; but for some reason, I wasn't lucky enough to be selected.

Teamwork is hard work

Teamwork can happen organically, but it also takes work, communication, and solid leadership. When the people you are responsible for work well together, the performance and culture is always positively impacted.

Here are some suggestions for managers and really anyone for making sure teamwork is optimized:

- Hire and recruit not to fill empty positions, but based on how individuals will compliment your existing team.
- Consider team-based interviewing to foster buy in and input of your current team on potential new team members.
- Facilitate team meetings at least twice a month to encourage cross-functional or departmental communication and updates.
- Develop a code of ethics with your team that everyone agrees to, and use this as your standard for communication, conflict resolution, and roadmap in working together.
- Focus on team recognition, in addition to individual recognition.
- Do not tolerate toxic and negative behaviors within your team, and address toxic people and issues immediately.

Finally, understanding what your team members need to be successful is also important. Take time to meet one-on-one regularly to check in and make sure that people are getting what they need from you.

Teams won't work well together unless the individual needs of their members are taken care of first.

Patience of a saint

The best way to make an instant impact when starting a new position, is to assess and listen only…at least for the first thirty days, but likely even longer.

The main goal when starting a new role as a leader should be to establish trust first with as many people as possible, and to understand and learn.

Resist the temptation to immediately implement new ideas and to make changes. Without truly knowing everything you should, premature changes and actions can wind up being a disaster and can alienate many who you need to be on your side in the long term.

Face value

Stop trying to seek acceptance, approval, and validation from people you will never receive it from.

It's a waste of time and energy.

You know who they are in your life.

Instead, build your own following and circle with people who are interested, appreciative, and encouraging of the value you bring to the table, and who you are.

This is ultimately a much more fulfilling, successful, and productive way to live and work.

Out of sight, out of mind

In the absence of true leadership, it's not uncommon for individuals to rally behind any person in an organization that emerges who is decisive, supportive, fair, and action-oriented.

What you might not expect is that person could be you.

Letting go of one for the team

I once had a "superstar" employee give me an ultimatum. He demanded that another employee in his department be terminated, or he was going to resign.

The other employee was new to his role, was making mistakes, and was frustrating the superstar as he felt it was impacting his performance. What the superstar didn't know, however, was that the person in question was getting rave reviews from customers and other employees, positively impacting the department, and showing great potential. And yes, was making mistakes, but nothing that couldn't be corrected with proper training.

After looking into the situation thoroughly, I decided to accept the superstar's resignation. His complaints were mostly unwarranted and was essentially seeking attention and attempting to display dominance and control over the rest of the team.

The bottom line is…no matter how high performing an employee is, nothing is worth allowing toxic behavior on a team. It sets a dangerous precedent and sends an unhealthy message—that negative behaviors and inappropriate demands are okay if someone is a top producer.

It was the right decision. The team was so grateful that they ultimately hit new highs in performance, grew stronger, reduced turnover, and morale improved greatly.

This scenario taught me that it's alright to never be held hostage by a top producer's tantrums, especially if they are a culture killer. It's never a good outcome.

Point blank

The most successful people I have worked with are always the ones who say to leadership what everyone else is thinking but may be too afraid to say.

Giving is much better than receiving

Over time, I have found that *demonstrating* loyalty to people is far more meaningful and gratifying than *demanding* loyalty from people.

Career ladder

Leadership is really a two-way street. In addition to knowing what teams need from a leader, it's important to consider what the best leaders need from their teams. Some of these needs include:

Teamwork: Leaders hope and pray that their best people work together and collaborate, not fight, backstab, and sabotage one another.

No surprises: Leaders expect their team members to be transparent, timely, and upfront with information, and like everyone, they really dislike surprises.

Leaders like to be challenged and not "yessed" to death. There is a high level of respect for team members who propose new and different ideas, solutions, and creative ways of thinking.

Solutions: Great leaders appreciate unvarnished feedback, but also appreciate that problems and challenges are accompanied by proposed solutions.

Attitude: A can-do, "I will get it done," attitude is very appealing and alluring to a leader, and often those who project this attitude are leaned on very heavily with responsibility and favored with career advancement opportunities.

Ability to elevate others: Leaders look for team members who can elevate the rest of the team. The best leaders are also able to attract people to work for them who have abilities that are at least equal to their own, and ideally even better.

Diversity: The best leaders understand, value, and celebrate having teams who are diverse in culture and backgrounds, and people who are not shy in using their unique perspective to elevate results.

Follow through and follow up: Nothing is appreciated more by a leader than to not have to chase individuals for follow-up, and they notice those who follow through consistently on their commitments.

Balance: Strong leaders expect and encourage their team members to not be workaholics and understand that the more balanced they are, the more effective they will be.

I am fortunate that I have gotten to work the majority of my career with individuals who demonstrate these qualities consistently. It makes a world of difference in morale, results, and more.

Working out the kinks

Some of my most valued professional relationships today are with people that I had adversarial relationships with earlier in my career.

It has taught me to never give up on people.

There are often situations and circumstances that bring people together, even people you do not get along with today, in a way you might not be able to foresee today.

These situations can forge invaluable and long-lasting relationships with people that you will need and rely upon. Those individuals may be one of your greatest resources for advice, support, and resources in your career.

Don't give up on people in your professional life that you have challenges with today. You might be cheating yourself of deep connections if you do.

There's no way around it

Always respect the chain of command in your organization. If you are communicating, managing, or engaging with employees, whether upstream, downstream, or those lateral to you, you can't bypass their direct reporting structure.

It creates resentment, confusion, and toxicity in a company culture. I see it occurring all the time in companies, and it never works. It is not worth it, it is wrong, and it is disrespectful to others.

Opportunity zones

You must invest in people if you expect them to have longevity in your company. You also have to invest in people so they develop others. And you have to invest in people so they stand out to your customers from the sea of competition.

Wanting vs. needing

Inspiration and motivation often occur when you least expect it.

I recently had lunch with a physician friend who is in his mid-70s. We somehow got on the topic of retirement, and he said, "I can't retire, I have to work."

I responded that I understood that finances and income are important, especially with unexpected expenses, inflation, etc.

He corrected me and said that he didn't *need* to work for money any longer and acknowledged he was fortunate to be in that position.

He then stated that he *wanted* to work because of the interaction with people, for the feeling of contributing something, and as he put it, "To feel alive."

That's what inspired me. When a person doesn't have to work but does because it is meaningful and they are passionate about it, that is a life to aspire to.

To me, that is what life is all about. Purpose, meaning, and making connections with people, regardless of your age.

May we all be this lucky.

Measuring tape

One of the key business indicators that I used to watch closely when I ran a large company was how many individuals would reach out to me or my team and ask to work for us.

I still use this as a barometer today of how well my own company is doing.

This is a good way to measure how talent views your company culture. No different than wanting consumers to choose your company for the product or service you offer.

There is a big difference between the act of recruiting people to your company vs. people seeking your company out as an employer.

This to me is a great reflection of how good a company is.

Words to live by

> It helps if you approach your work every day with:
> A clear mind,
> An open heart,
> A collaborative spirit,
> An empathetic soul,
> A competitive drive,
> An iron will,
> A calm temperament,
> A good sense of humor,
> A healthy self-awareness,
> A humble personality,
> And a really, really good attitude.

Togetherness

Company conferences are a great and important way to establish and communicate core messages with employees. Many companies do this on an annual basis and gather their leaders together to set the tone for the year.

It reminds me of the many, many company leadership conferences, retreats, and meetings I have planned and led over the years. I have always put a lot of time and effort into trying to craft meaningful, educational, and inspiring events and content for team members.

Here is the reality though…

What employees value the most at these conferences and meetings is spending time with their coworkers.

The chance to get to know peers better, share war stories, learn from one another, and have an enjoyable time together, is really what people look forward to and appreciate.

No matter how good your event speakers are, the quality of your agenda, the activities you have planned…people will enjoy and remember spending time with each other more than anything.

If the goal is to make your teams feel really good about your company through a conference or a retreat, keep this in mind and you will accomplish just that.

House rules

From time to time, I think about the first real "boss" that I had who I knew was also a real leader. She told me she had a few simple rules for me and everyone else that worked for her:

- "I don't like surprises."
- "I am not a babysitter."
- "I am not a micromanager, but don't take advantage of this."

She turned out to be a great mentor and manager, and she really lived by these rules. Now as a manger myself, these rules are just as relevant and important to me today as they were thirty years ago.

Just show it!

Words can express your gratitude, but actions are what truly show it.

To do list

If you are a manager who is responsible for multiple people in multiple locations, here are some tips to help foster trust from your teams:

1. Visit your teams on their turf. Don't drag them to a corporate office which is overly stressful for many and can kill an entire day. Try also to limit the number of virtual meetings that you request their presence on. Unless critical, they will wind up impersonal, annoying, and unproductive.

2. Respect people's time by scheduling your visits, and always be punctual. Drop-in and last-minute meetings and visits should be reserved for emergencies.
3. Be thoughtful. Bring something with you on your visit, even if it is as simple as a cup of coffee or donuts.
4. Ignore your texts, email, and phone calls when visiting with team members in person.
5. Spend more time listening than talking.
6. Compliment team members when with them.
7. Check in with people on an appropriate personal topic when you visit them. All work or all business is a turn off.
8. Send a follow-up thank you message after a meeting…text is fine, email is better, handwritten note is best.

If you think this is overkill, I encourage you to reconsider. This is what people mean when they talk about the culture of a company.

Brief but important

It's good to remember that difficult never means impossible.

Keep in touch

Recruiting talent requires persistence *and* patience. Sometimes you know what is better for someone before they can see it for themselves. But they have to see it for themselves to act.

There have been people I have discussed career options with one, two, and even three years ago who wound up not making a job change at the time. But by staying in touch, checking in routinely, and following their careers closely, they will contact you when they are ready. And everyone at some point is ready for something new.

The key is to have the candidate's best interest at heart. If you truly are driven by helping people find the best possible position for them, they will know it and trust you, and they will always turn to you for guidance and direction.

Goals of good leadership

I have never met or worked with a person who was passionate about achieving goals that someone else established for them.

People have to set their own goals to be excited and accountable about reaching them.

There are goals.

There are "stretch" goals.

And there are unrealistic goals.

Most individuals set their own goals and believe they can reach them, and often do.

Good managers and leaders help and encourage team members to reach stretch goals. Many people underestimate what they are capable of, and good leadership should assist them in getting there.

Unrealistic goals are unattainable generally and demoralizing. They do more damage than they do good.

The right seat on the bus

I have always viewed a manager's job to understand, accept, and compensate, when needed, for their team members' weaknesses.

The more important responsibility, though, is to understand and recognize team members' strengths, and to make sure they are involved in activities and projects that allow them to soar with those strengths.

It's all in the details

I have interviewed hundreds of people in my career for various roles at this point. While I always try to be very present in the moment and give informative interviews, I do regret one bad habit that I have had for many years.

That habit was not following up with candidates who did not get the position for which they were interviewing.

It's a bad habit, but not a malicious one. Many hiring managers just find the right candidate and typically move on from there and forget or don't prioritize follow-up.

But I started correcting this a few years ago and found that people are very appreciative when you close the loop with them. Especially when the feedback regarding the interview is constructive and intended to help them with their interviewing skills, their resume, or offering general suggestions to improve their chances for the next opportunity they pursue.

The bonus…

People remember kindness. Often you cross paths with these candidates at various stages in their career and they become the perfect candidates for something you are recruiting for later on.

I try to remember that feeling of not knowing what went wrong in an interview when you do not hear back. I have been there, it can be unsettling. But now I try to make it unnecessary for people.

The genius bar

A person who is a genius in their field is perceived as average if they cannot communicate well.

A person who is of average intelligence in their field, is perceived as a genius to others if they can communicate well.

The reason is that the communicator adds incredible value to others, and the genius adds very little if they are a poor communicator.

Houston, we have a problem!

Conflict resolution is an art. I have fumbled many times as a manager when it comes to this topic, but the upside is the challenging situations helped me to improve.

One thing is for sure, conflict resolution is a constant dynamic in the workplace, regardless of what side of the conflict you may end up on.

The following are some tips and suggestions I have learned by trial and error regarding this important topic:

- Never take sides.
- Remember your role as a leader is to seek common ground and compromise, not fault.
- Understand each person's point of view and consult with them one-on-one first to assess their side.
- Accept that in high-performance cultures conflict is always certain.
- Assess how others on the periphery view this conflict without disclosing sensitive information.
- Address the conflict as quickly as possible. When you avoid a conflict, it can be far worse than the conflict itself.
- You can ask the involved parties to resolve the conflict on their own, and present to you the resolution, but this can be risky and often doesn't do the trick unless it is a simple conflict.
- The preferred approach is to meet with all the parties after you have done most of the above steps.
- At the meeting, establish ground rules, articulate you are not judging, but just facilitating. State that your goal is to resolve the conflict. Ask each side to respect one another's perspective, and let all parties know that you respect and value everyone at the table equally.
- Let each side address one another.
- Ask those involved what their suggested resolution is. This is the key part of the meeting and people already know the answer in advance of the meeting.
- Always do everything on this list in person.

It's most important to let people produce their own resolution vs. you prescribing one. They will be more accountable to their own action plan. You should jump in if things get too heated or emotional and work to keep the conversation centered on resolution. Also, ask how you can help with the resolution and suggest ways to prevent the issues from occurring again. Suggest a meeting in a few weeks to monitor progress.

Every situation is different obviously, but this approach has worked for me 90 percent of the time, and the issues get resolved and people move on.

For the 10 percent of the time these suggestions may not work, it is a wise suggestion to refer the parties to human resources and have it worked out there.

Moving forward

In your career...

You will go up, sideways, down, in circles, fast, slow, with others, alone, and many other directions.

But the most important thing is to never, ever, go backward.

Air quality

Fear, insecurity, and doubt only exist when you give them oxygen.

You have control.

Going the distance

Intuition, luck, good timing, strong connections, a positive attitude, emotional intelligence, experience, and hard work all contribute greatly to success in business.

But none of these even come close to the success you achieve by never giving up. It's the most important of all.

The blame game

Often in business, true success in your career comes from knowing and understanding the difference between taking ownership and accountability for mistakes and problems instead of finding someone or something else to blame for them.

Give and take

As you develop and grow your professional inner circle, it's important to understand the character and intentions of people.

Over time, you come to realize there are people who seek your help and guidance, and then there are people who want to or need something from you.

People who seek your help and guidance often do this out of respect, trust, and admiration. That is a good thing.

People who "want" something from you, are often seeking to use you or your connections and knowledge, without regard to your best interest or benefit.

It's key to understand the difference between both in your career.

Room for growth

Bonafide success comes from never being the smartest person in the room. If you are, you're surrounding yourself with the wrong people.

Going out on top

It's always best to search for a new job when you are at peak performance in your current position.

Looking for a new job when you are the most secure, performing well, and at the top of your game accomplishes three key things:

1. You will have more and better-quality employer options.
2. You will command a higher salary.
3. You won't leave with brain fog or any baggage knowing that the choice to leave was 100 percent yours and that you left on your terms.

Same concept when seeking an internal promotion.

It is not easy to uproot yourself when you are doing well in a position and comfortable, but from personal experience, it is the best way to open up better opportunities.

Using a compass

There is a fine line, yet a big difference between…
Confidence vs. arrogance
Listening vs. hearing
Empathy vs. pity
Aggressiveness vs. assertiveness
Being opinionated vs. being tone-deaf
A leader vs. a tyrant
Your convictions vs. your actions
Knowing the difference between each in your actions and those people to associate with will go a long way in your career quality.

The tightrope

The best marketing is part science, part magic and part artistry.
A key driver of success I have learned in marketing is knowing when to pull back and be subtle and knowing when to be "full on" and visible.

A teaching moment

The moment you realize that you are gratified more by the success of your team vs. your own success, is the moment you become a leader.

It's never too late

I don't believe anyone who says they have no regrets.
As long as we are alive, everyone has a chance to address and eliminate their regrets. Denying that you have them, also denies you the opportunity to fix them.

Image is everything

You are *known* for something. Whether you care or not, think about it or not, or know it or not, you are known for something.

That something will dictate a lot in your career. It will dictate who chooses to work with and for you, the opportunities presented to you, the level and amount of respect you receive, and will dictate your professional fulfillment. Solicit feedback on this more from people you trust. It is worthwhile. It is not narcissistic, it's your reputation.

Many times, what we think that we are known for is not what others think at all. You have total control over this, but it requires work and effort. Work hard on this and think about it often.

Free advice

The most meaningful things you can do for your career costs nothing:

- Learning through reading, coaching from mentors, taking on new projects, etc.
- Do the work everyone else avoids, especially "heavy-lift" and unglamorous projects. The right people will notice.
- Avoid negative people!
- Stick to your values in every decision you make.
- Help others without a "quid pro quo" expectation.
- Show up when least expected for someone.
- Give credit to others, take less for yourself.
- Develop and elevate others.

All fail proof, all free.

Tough calls

I have had the good fortune in my career of helping to build companies from infancy stage to sizable and meaningful brands.

Scaling a company can be daunting, challenging, and yet a very exciting endeavor.

It may mean turning down opportunities when you don't feel your company has the bandwidth, it may mean stretching and taking on new projects and clients when you are already stretched too thin, and it might require building and investing in your infrastructure before you have the business to support it.

I think the most important factor in growing correctly though is ensuring that your culture is well defined, the people who work with and for you share your values and vision, and your mission is carried out in everything you do, so that quality of work is never compromised.

Multiplicity

It's best to avoid people who disparage others, especially when they disparage people that they appear or pretend to be close with.

Odds are if they disparage these people so easily, they will do the same to you, and might in fact already be doing it.

Packing for your trip

Sometimes, I get creative bursts on long flights when I have that rare chance to not be distracted by my electronic devices. The following is an example of this...

Underrated career hacks not to forget:

- *Practice balance*: Lead yourself first and foremost.
- *Health first, career second*: Physical and mental fitness are crucial in achieving results and fulfillment.
- *Be unselfish*: With your time, your ideas, and your recognition of others.
- *Self-awareness*: Know your strengths, and really know your weaknesses.
- *Don't personalize things*: Business is business, and don't tolerate anyone who attempts to makes things personal with you.

- *Be punctual*: You parents were right after all.
- *Avoid "yes" people*: People who challenge you are your real allies.
- *Apologize more*: Own it when you are wrong; it shows character and strength more than anything else.
- *Be an open book*: Being vulnerable and transparent builds trust with others.
- *Be consistent*: People follow leaders who don't vacillate in their approach, their values, and their judgment.
- *Follow through on commitments*: Always do what you promise others you will do. If you can't, don't promise.
- *Humor*: Be human with people, laugh a little with them and at your own expense, not anyone else's.

Let nature take its course

Never hold someone back from a promotion they deserve because it will be hard to replace them in their current role.

I had this happen to me early in my career, the company that I worked for didn't want to rock the boat with things going so well in the role I was in, and instead gave me a nice raise to appease me.

But it wasn't about the money for me, and I suspect most people feel the same.

Ambitious people want to grow. If you don't develop them and allow them to advance, they will seek out a company that will.

Game over

I always think that without a strong company culture, an organization is like a soccer or hockey team that doesn't have a goalie in front of the net. You have no protection or insurance that your employees feel appreciated or will be loyal.

It's open season for your competitors to score against you at any moment.

Setting up for failure?

Performance improvement plans (PIPs) don't work. They are usually aimed at setting an employee for failure. When employees don't perform, it is more likely that leadership is weak, there is no competent coaching program in place, morale is low, and people are hired for positions they are either not prepared for or are in the wrong seat on the bus.

There are much more effective ways to address concerns with employees than this dated approach. A savvy human resources department can guide organizations to implement a more purposeful program.

Lifting others up

One of the true hallmarks of a successful career is the number of people that you manage who move on to greater things in their career. As that list grows, so should your confidence and fulfillment as a manager and a leader.

Class is in session

The ABCs of attracting talent:

An employer with an A-list culture and an A-list product or service will attract A-list talent.

An employer with an A-list culture who has a B-, C-, or even D-list product or service will attract A-list talent. The talent knows the employer will support them and do what it takes to improve the product or service.

An employer with a B-, C-, or D-list culture who has an A-list product or service will have trouble finding A-list talent. The talent knows that bad culture eventually trickles to the core business.

An employer with a B-, C-, or D-list culture with a B-, C-, or D-list product or service will not survive long.

Finding your niche

You can build a meaningful and successful business by being an alternative to what everyone else in the market is offering.

You don't have to be the biggest, you don't have to have the highest market share, and you don't have to be the most well-known to thrive. Customers crave non-cookie cutter options.

What you do have to ensure is that you serve your clients better, offer a unique value proposition, and over deliver. People will notice this. The key is personalization and being as hands on as possible. This can be hard to achieve for many large organizations, but not impossible.

Success isn't defined by how large an organization is, rather how good an organization is. Quality over quantity can be a game changer.

Balancing act

Teach yourself that what you consider to be your greatest weaknesses, are also your greatest strengths. It really is true, and this mindset can help you navigate those moments and days when you doubt yourself.

For example, if you tend to think out of the box often but work in an environment that is somewhat rigid and very structured, remember that you see things that others do not, which is a rare and incredible skill to have.

Another example is if you take it hard when things don't go your way, this can also be indicative of aspiring to perfection and great ambition, which is a highly common trait shared by the most successful people.

And if you often feel anxious while the rest of the world seemingly has everything under control, don't worry. This means that you have a tenacious sense of urgency and like to accomplish things, and not just talk about them.

It's all about perspective, and I encourage anyone reading this to remember this thought when you need to.

Playing by ear

No one teaches you how to be intuitive.
No one can tell you how to be compassionate.
No one can really prepare you for the challenges you never expected.
No one shows you how to keep your attitude positive.
No one can train you to be humble.
No one provides you with a road map for your life.
And no one forces you to make the decisions that you make.
We can be influenced and encouraged in all these areas, but it's ultimately up to us to choose how we conduct ourselves. Nobody else.

Can I see a job description?

In my experience, most people, including me, spend at least 50 percent of their time at work involved in things not in their job description.
There is a word for this. Teamwork.

Free as a bird

The most valuable people to surround yourself with professionally are those who are untethered, unincumbered, and non-beholden to anyone. They always tell it like it is.

Raise your hand if you agree

Someone asked me this week for advice in asking for a raise. I told them I was the wrong person to ask, I never asked for a raise in my entire career.
I suggested that anyone worth working for would proactively engage in a discussion about salary at least annually. I also shared that if you are hardworking, add value and stand out, you will never have to ask for a raise, fair compensation should occur organically.

Choose your battles

When it comes to recruiting talent to your company, some advice: Don't chase people. If someone makes it too difficult to recruit them, the odds are that even if you are successful in recruiting them to work for you, these situations rarely work out.

Instead, put your energy into strong candidates who want to work for and appreciate what your organization has to offer them. The potential for success is much better for both your company and the employee when someone is eager and ready to join!

Nonnegotiables

I have spent a large part of my career on the marketing, sales, and business development side of business.

I have found that there are some essential rules in these areas if you want to realize true success:

- Never overpromise and always over deliver.
- Embrace modern technology to strengthen your brand and to help drive awareness.
- Know thyself and differentiate your brand strongly. Avoid a cookie cutter approach.
- Never be the most expensive, nor the cheapest.
- Utilize your current customers as your ambassadors.
- Your internal customers are as important as your external customers.
- Make it easy for customers to do business with you and seek their feedback frequently.
- Resolve complaints quickly.
- Know your competition inside and out.
- Reinvent your brand often. Customers get bored with the same old, same old.

The front of the line

In my experience, the best ideas in any company originate from the people on the front line doing the work. Rarely do they come from a corporate directive.

Companies with a healthy culture identify, support, nurture, and develop these ideas and initiatives which differentiate them and insulate them from failure.

Save some trees

For the last forty people or so that I have hired, I didn't request or look at their resumes. I realized a while ago that there is nothing on a resume that a person can't share more effectively in person.

And more importantly, if you are really recruiting team members to win, you learn and gauge more from an individual in speaking and meeting with them in person than can ever be captured or conveyed on a resume.

I have just come to believe that resumes are pointless these days.

I've got this

I have had a rule for most of my career when it comes to terminating employees. When someone who reports to me, is a peer, or who I report to suggests, insists, or politics me to fire a direct report of mine, I say, "Who do you have lined up to replace that person?"

99.9 percent of the time…*crickets*.

In other words, unless you have a better solution or person, don't worry about it, I've got this. Obvious and unavoidable situations notwithstanding, the best leaders stand by the people they believe in. That's how successful companies are built.

Conflicts and politicking are natural and common in every organization, courage…not so much.

Late bloomers

If you are attempting something new to differentiate your company, don't get discouraged if the new idea doesn't take off immediately.

Be patient.

Many game-changing innovative ideas that are slow to gain traction are often what many will be trying to copy a year or two down the line.

The good news for the idea creator…it is extremely hard to replicate the original.

Raise the bar

Pursue success for the sake of your own personal fulfillment and satisfaction.

Ambition driven by revenge or to prove a point to someone else is not healthy and a waste of time.

Succeeding because you raised the bar for yourself, translates into much more meaningful and inspiring results. If you can do this, you have already succeeded.

At the end of the day…

Perspective is an incredibly powerful tool in business, leadership, and life in general.

Increasingly, I have been thinking that if I am worried today about a professional challenge or problem that in five years will have no meaning or relevance to me or anyone else, I will quickly move on from it.

This mindset has really helped me prioritize and focus on what's important and let go easier of the distractions that can hinder progress and forward movement.

Ground rules

When it comes to new ideas that team members share, I have two core rules I try to always follow and require others to follow:

No. 1: Never propose a new idea unless you are prepared to own it.
No. 2: If an idea is shared in a meeting among team members, no one is allowed to shut down the idea or criticize it, unless they offer one in return.

The first one forces thought into action, the second one eliminates the idea crushers (there are a few on every team). Both work very well in my experience!

The devil's in the details

Pay attention to and respect the devil's advocates on your teams, network, and professional circle. On the surface, these folks can seem negative and rebellious, but often they are saying what a lot of people are thinking but are hesitant to say. They are only looking out for you and/or the company's best interest.

Their feedback can be constructive and pivotal to ensuring the right decisions are made and huge mistakes are avoided. But you must check your ego at the door. Surrounding yourself with only "yes people" can be tempting and make you feel good but can lead to many problems and failures.

Filtering

The managers and leaders who I've worked for that I have respected the most in my career, are the ones who never passed along the pressure or stress they were receiving from above them to their teams.

I have seen people do this exceptionally well, and it is a very underrated, yet unbelievably valuable skill in any organization.

The power of one

It only takes one…
One person who thanks you for your contribution to the team.
One person who tells you that they love your idea and to run with it.
One person who shares how appreciative they are of you.
One person who encourages you to always reach your potential.
One person who tells you that they have total confidence in your ability to succeed.

Try to be that one person for someone every day. It can make a difference in so many ways to your team's performance, morale, and the overall culture in your work environment.

Good leaders do this in the best of times.
The best leaders do this always.

It's all on you

If you recruit a colleague who you are close with to join your company, it is your responsibility to ensure their success, especially during their first year. Yes, they must perform well, but ultimately the employee is joining your organization because they trust you and your judgment.

If you cannot ensure that they will be secure in their position at your company and that you will have their back, you should not recruit people to whom you are close with.

This is an especially important factor in developing your reputation and developing relationships in the industry that you work in.

A compliment or an insult?

This happens a lot. A colleague recently told me he started a new job, and his former company hired multiple new people and promoted two others to take on his former responsibilities.

My response was, "If you left a company for a new opportunity, don't be angry or annoyed if you have been replaced by several people."

I shared that he should think of it as a compliment that he was able to accomplish a lot (and more) as one person vs. what numerous people have been hired or promoted to do after he left.

What happens in a pinch?

When selecting a vendor, partner, supplier, etc. in business, I always ask a question that takes people by surprise but have found that it is the most important question to ask.

The response I receive to this question is the deciding factor in choosing what vendor to select.

And it's a simple question, "What happens when there is a problem, how will you handle it with us, and what is your process?"

You can really tell a lot about an organization by how well and how authentically this question is answered.

My best advice

> Here is some advice on giving advice:
> Be honest with your advice.
> Be constructive with advice, not critical.
> Put yourself in the other person's shoes.
> Encourage people to follow their gut instinct always.
> Don't advise on what you know nothing about
> Encourage the person to consider all sides of an issue or opportunity.
> Make sure you know exactly what the person's goal is.
> Don't be offended if your advice is not taken.

Don't say a word about this

The best sales coaching I ever received was:
When you meet with someone for the first time, say nothing about your company or what you have to offer for at least the first twenty to thirty minutes. It forces you to ask and listen.

It is a game changer.

Connect the dots

Although it is not always obvious, the smartest individual in your company is the person who hired the person that you admire the most in your company.

Stretch goals

Successful companies back up the promises they make to their customers.

If you are ever told by a supervisor to not overpromise to potential or existing customers, you may be working in an environment that has an underdeliver mindset and that is worrisome.

The winning formula is always when the customer is satisfied more than they expected to be.

Look inward first

If an employee resigns to work for a competitor, don't blame the competitor for "poaching" your employee.

Redirect your energy to find out why the employee was vulnerable and easy to recruit by the competitor in the first place, what you can do to retain them, and what you can do to prevent similar situations from occurring again.

At the end of the day, a strong culture is your best defense to prevent employees from leaving or even entertaining a conversation with a new employer.

True blue

You don't have to change who you are to be successful.

The more authentic and truer you are to yourself; the more people will notice and want to be around you and want to do business with you.

And those who may not gravitate toward you…don't sweat it. They may be struggling to be themselves but haven't gotten there yet. When they do, they might return to your orbit.

Some fuel for your journey…

Some realities and advice regarding careers:

- Nothing is a dress rehearsal. Every second counts, everything you do matters and impacts your next step.
- The best people to work for judge you by the contributions you make over time, not a moment in time.
- The past can't be changed, but you will cheat yourself if you don't learn from it.
- What you say matters, what you do matters more.
- No one ever gets ahead by not taking smart risks.
- Count your blessings every day for what you have achieved, while challenging yourself to accomplish more.
- The greatest gift in business is what you create and get done with others, and the relationships you develop as a result.
- Seek trust from others more than anything, this is a must in achieving success.
- Everything is your choice and your control; don't allow anyone to make you feel differently.
- Focus more on what you give than what you get, and you will receive more without even trying.
- Let go of animosity and revenge, karma will take care of it all ultimately.

Most importantly…take care of yourself first, so you can be your best for those who rely on you to be in top form.

Parting thoughts

Change is essential to success in anyone's career.

A good rule of thumb to ask yourself is, "How different is what I am doing today from what I was doing a year ago?"

If the answer is not that much, you should consider challenging yourself to try novel approaches, learn new information and skills, and try things that scare you a little.

Otherwise, the worst thing can happen…you will become stagnant.

Human nature encourages all of us too often to seek a comfort zone. There is no shame in this. But everyone owes it to themselves to stretch their abilities and evolve.

If you do not challenge yourself to evolve, change, and grow, someone else might.

Choose to do it on your own terms!

ABOUT THE AUTHOR

Tim Hodges is an experienced leader with over thirty years of experience in the health-care industry. He has spent his entire career advocating and working to improve the quality of care for older adults.

Tim started his career in the hospital sector of health-care working in government relations and transitioned to leadership roles in operations and marketing for some of the largest senior care organizations in the United States.

Tim currently is the cofounder and CEO of Honor Aging, a strategic advisory firm in the health-care industry. He is also a member of the American Diabetes Association Community Leadership Board and enjoys traveling and supporting the performing arts and animal rights organizations.